Human Rites

E.A. Markham

Human Rites

SELECTED POEMS 1970-1982

Anvil Press Poetry

Published in 1984
by Anvil Press Poetry Ltd
69 King George Street London SE10 8PX
ISBN 0 85646 112 1 (hardback)
      0 85646 113 X (paperback)

*This book is published with
financial assistance from
The Arts Council of Great Britain*

Photoset in Melior
by Bryan Williamson, Todmorden
Printed and bound in Great Britain
by The Camelot Press Ltd, Southampton

FOR DIANA

NOTE AND ACKNOWLEDGEMENTS

The *Lambchops* selection is more or less arbitrary; we had about eighty poems from which to choose. *Lambchops* sprang to life on the poetry-reading circuit in the mid-1970s, and appeared in various little magazines and collections (*Lambchops*, Omens, 1976; *Lambchops in Disguise*, Share Publications, 1976; *Philpot in the City*, Curlew Press, 1976) under the authorship of Paul St Vincent. Only when they are reprinted, as here, do I reclaim them as my own.

Acknowledgements are due to the following magazines and anthologies, books and pamphlets in which other poems first appeared: *Ambit, Bluefoot Traveller, Delta, Gallery, Kunapipi, Limestone, The Literary Review, Melanthika, Only Poetry, PN Review, Poetry Durham, Poetry Review, Race Today, Tribune* and *Wormwood Review; Cross-fire* (Outposts, 1972), *Games & Penalties* (Poet & Printer, 1980), *The Lamp* (Sceptre Press, 1978), *Love Poems* (Lobby Press, 1978), *Love, Politics & Food* (Von Hallett, 1982) and *Mad* (Aquila/The Phaethon Press, 1973). Some poems have also been broadcast by ABC, BBC Radio and Radio London.

E.A.M.

CONTENTS

1 West Indian Myths

West Indian Myth 1

In the beginning was Man
standing still, Man in a hurry

hunting new skins in London
like Man beginning late.

In the beginning was evening,
White Studies on the State trapping

Man, breast-feeding, thigh-
beating him into mess, submission—his body

blackening with the victory scars.
In the beginning Man wrapped his past

in Community Relations like a left-
over bandage to entertain his friends;

and after all the fun, he ended up
years later, right where he began.

West Indian Myth 2

We don't sing Brother, we don't play the coon
We storm the fort with intellect, with dialectic cool.

International travellers, we smash the native barrier
With skill and flexibility of the licensed degree-carrier.

We spread the word in approved tongues and helpful thighs
For we are your alternative to hypocrisies, jealousies and
　　lies:

We're not your common, vulgar, phrase-book sort
We bring you Mao, Marcuse—even J.-P. Sartre on Art.

So when the show is over and Madame invites to disrobe her
'he who could greet you in Swahili and say goodbye in
　　Yoruba',

How dare the upstart, 'Power to Baader-Meinhof' louts
The 'ça va, ça va, alle ist klar baby, alle ist klar' touts

Jump the queue and leave you scrambling for the dictionary
Like a twopenny-ha'penny, centime, pfennig nobody.

West Indian Myth 3

I am not a mugger, madam,
as you can see by my dress and

(excuse me, you won't be needing these
any more) manners. Note that my teeth

are all my own freshly brushed
and not blackened by obscene language.

Let me kiss you as the lover of your
choice (I am not, you see, prejudiced,

though a male chauvinist by persuasion
and clumsy with animals). One more thing:

I have misplaced my identity
with my card and must give you this

(forgive me) and this and this to know me by
when vengeance comes, when you are hysterical.

West Indian Myth 4

Third-generation poem recording
the trip, skirmishes, decades

of neglect. Mutation and revision
still accord it a link

with prehistory.
Prehistory is a joke in a library book

granting the status of fossil
to a newly-composed text, heavy

with apology, with deaths
to make itself seem real.

West Indian Myth 5

A grandson distances, reconnects
the house to torn memory.

You will drift back, near-parasite,
to this now strategic outpost.

Here, where once was city,
raw waves break upon the shore: gulls,

ships, whiff of long-
abandoned family force obedience

out of you, out of all. Fact
will not dissolve into Myth

as you plead old age, incompetence.
For dying will be harder.

West Indian Myth 6

And tourists came to the hot island
to smell native armpits, to screw

in the fields, while god sent
foreign storms and earthquakes

to puritanize the Myth. So the drought
that followed was well done.

Now holiday-island exiles slum it
in the cities of their dreams, sniffing

at old armpits, ready for the thug
of hurricane, of earthquake

disguised as the natives.

The Boy of the House

The ruin of the house, he lies on his stomach, womanless.
The boy is in water, frog-like, his mouth tastes of
   sea-weed.
He is looking at the rose-garden, it's not there
No longer at the front of the house—
Of what used to be the house...

The rose-garden is now at the bottom of the sea
And the boy throws a line, then another
To prevent more of the house drifting away.
He does this instead of growing into middle-age, or going
   abroad:
The boy is a great source of worry.

The Man Who Stayed at Home

He sits at home looking at the mountains.
He hears a young girl practising her scales.
Snap, say the tourists
taking him back to Boston, to Hamburg

to colour the winter. Sagging, on his verandah, the man
is all that's left of this once-great house
where no one learned to play the piano—
Chekhov of the tropics, say the tourists.

He waits for heirs
to return from the North with plunder and confidence
to rebuild, their link with this place unbroken:
will they use heads or hands for this?

The man watches and dreams of reunion
with the concert pianist reclaiming her instrument,
as familiar mountains edge closer
thinking him last of his line.

Seconds

Though they called themselves SECOND THOUGHTS
they knew what they were. They were *seconds*.

Raymond was the second son, Franco was pipped
at the post in the 800 yards that mattered

and Max *just* failed to win the Island Scholarship.
From runner-up to hand-me-down is a fate

few escape, so the lads decided to organize
a future. It grew to fill up the middle part

of their lives, like long walks after dinner
against the traffic. They had planned

their Revolution and were ready,
their second thoughts told them they were ready.

All that was needed was to wait, to wait
till the Firsts went ahead and had failed;

so the Seconds though ready, waited, secure
in their positions, like people in a book.

Inheritance

The topless native
of our ship trusts
her blue eyes
for she knows already
how this trip will end.

And I half-believe
her, barely doubt
the dog-eared
evidence from a diary
she will publish.

She says it all: she
knows the man I'm
on my way to be. My
predecessors have armed her
with my secrets.

Roots, Roots

My grandmother's donkey had a name
I can't recall. It's not important
for the donkey, a beast of burden
like my grandmother, is dead.
And I am in a different place.

Perhaps the donkey was a horse, a status symbol
or a man, married to my grandmother;
and he lives on with my name.
But then, suppose there was no donkey,
no grandmother, no other place?

2 Love Poems

Accident

It is no accident
this accident
a lost wife
in the lift
day after day—
the smile today
straying some way past
recognition.
Tomorrow, preened
I shall make
amends. Tomorrow
will our fray
commence. What
if the happy run
of accidents
proves tomorrow
an accident?
I shall curse
the memory; and
when the memory
starts to please—
I shall be old.

The Kiss

She opened her bag with the scented tissue
And asked for his mouth.
And there in the street she bathed it like her own
For he had been dreaming of her, had tasted her
In that last hour before she was clean.
And the scum of her bath was wiped from his lips
Which left them naked; so she applied the kiss.

Love Poem

Part of the hand copying this
traps a warmish glow of memory
inside its clasp—and daren't

let go. Out of prudence, I offer
this time, less of Self
than before, whittled

by the random edge of absence.
Fun, though, to revisit an old scene:
a southern escapade, living

in light others paint by, together
humouring the flesh. Ignore my foot.
Like a poor relation stiffening

with resentment, it protests
but stands firm under the body's
settling—don't ask it to dance.

So there we are, my love.
Not enemies: no hint of John Donne
writing your sonnet to a wife

dead of her twelfth confinement,
no after-divorce jollity, even:
take care now, there's love in that.

Love in a New Language

She is upstairs learning the language.
He must pause on the landing, give her time.
They have come through borders,
by accident saying the right thing, hitching
over danger, walking along motorways;
soon they will breakfast on the *Terasse*
be again rich without money.
Nearing the fourth floor, little flag
of achievement ready, he discounts
others who gained high ground before him
returning without fanfare: a trick
to limit custom to the regulars.
The pack on his back shifts, settles
on a too-recent bruise of caution:
she will prove a slow learner, halting him
on the stairs for years, decades. That
little joke they will share
when she has showered, and donned the language.

Then, with a slip of the tongue, she will unbuckle him.

A 'Late' Love Poem

He is older, lets
more of it pass: your
flavour

is unique, she says:
a pity to waste it.
He is puzzled

that millions
of *uniques*
sustaining her

fail to dissolve
into blandness.
There's hope for him, then.

He lets more of it
pass. A pity, she says:
A tragedy

not to have tasted it.

The Lamp

It was a graduation present, she had said—
these ten pieces of wood—all those New York
years ago. We had intended to assemble
it in London, in Stockholm; then in Paris found
that a screw was missing. But we were part
of the house, nevertheless, the one of the future
which would make sense of all these bits and pieces.

Now, rummaging through old boxes to discover
what could be reclaimed, I find our ten
wooden sticks, like a second-hand bargain.
The bestower of our gift is dead, her unspoken
fears long confirmed by everyone but two
stubborn nomads, reluctant to talk about it.
Some boxes later, I find more pieces

of lamp—one of them stamped No. 18. I begin
to accuse the Continents and the years.

Hello Again—Out of Season

Give it up, this hankering
for the world to be younger than us,
we must waive the right to give things their names:
this notion, slow-developing
like a tenacious illness
might ripen into something dangerous
while we age.
That's why we must act out of season,
late in the year: the old tendency
of waiting for the right time
has not paid off.

So I will give up trains.
Elsewhere, people like us are playing games with their
    children.
Not like us.
Your last trip away has blighted the trains.
Alone, in a carriage tactlessly reserved
you glide backwards out of the city
into a night of months.
How many times must we repay these moments?

Months have a habit of attracting years, decades.
People we know are getting rheumatism
and planning marriage for their children.
Those who speak for us are giving things their names.
They make trees sprout death
to punish our negligence.

Poised on that high wire of pride
between anger and guilt, we might have crossed
while earlier things were on offer.
Now we need protective armour
like the frail in power who overwhelm us with violence
and strut in our consent.

Allies on the ground will urge
with authority of the wounded
that we stay a little longer exposed
in gratitude to those playing games with their children,
in defiance of those who protect us with violence.

And who knows what this might bring?

A Good Life Sonnet

And all in all it's been a good life
(Not just to have outlived the sane, clever people)
But to have settled down finally with someone else's wife.
In the fog, we stood waiting for the bus
(I know, in Venice it would be on water)
But Archway in January was romantic enough for us.
She slipped her fortunes through my arm
Scarved herself to yashmak lest the harm

Of seeing too soon what the fog concealed
Prevent what proximity would soon have sealed.
So we stayed loyal to the fancy that brought us together
And released stray families from their vows of forever.
And all in all it's been a good life
To have brought my bad taste home to someone else's wife.

from Love Poems (1978)

i

Towards the end
of a non-earning week
of the year, I come
to meet you with flowers
in your mind.
Love defeats oldmaidenish
drizzle and is vindicated
as the 49 bus glides
through my second thoughts.
You're not on it, of course—
my lover, with a vengeance.

ii

You cross the minefield
climb the fence and
there she is doing
soft things behind
a curtain. The Lady is without
bodyguard. You break into
her dream and damage forever
her line of fantasy. Face
to blemished face you accuse
the other of unfair advantage,
of the vulgar wish to win. But
retreat is too high-
minded; so you agree: to exchange
weapons and carry on the fight
is the only thing to do.

*

Remote control draws
him past her and back again
till they meet

and then she defies him
thrusting her four legs
to the ground

and in reverse, in revenge
clawing at the ceiling,
her cries getting worse.

vi   (a dialogue)

You're good (theatre seats
with breasts) to touch;
your dreams (men on horseback
at the flat-warming, parting singly
at dawn) promote
my bestsellers' list.
You accept me as I am (night-
prowler, black-mailer, whole
football teams in disguise).
That's why I love you.

          *

I'm the collapsed breast
and spreading armpit
of your youth. You once failed
to check it with promises.
Now we swap tales of young
lovers whose rough tongues
assault our charitable meat.

viii

Why are we always low
on butter? she said, directing
his gaze elsewhere,
a little nervous of success
so late in life.
Not late, his eyes challenged,
just one of those delayed
mornings when you repeatedly
discover in yesterday's bread,
memories to toast.

ix

The morning after
we take turns to confess
little middle-aged illnesses
which lodge with us
like uninvited guests
stretching our tolerance.
After this meeting of—
what we in our playful way call—
minds, we agree
to share the medicine cabinet,
to take turns to fill
our prescriptions
and to relax, gradually
into second-best behaviour.

An Old Thought for a New Couple

She is not sure
if her failure
was important.

Death strikes
at his eyes again.
He puts on his glasses

and her smile returns.

3 Life after Spéracèdes

Life after Spéracèdes

for Diana

1

'Y'all take care, y'hear!'—Man in a Boston liquor store

I am writing from a new address.
You, too, are stranger to your apartment. So much
has changed since last year. To friends

we're apart in much the same way as before,
except that a year, coming between us,
has allowed ego to burn grey

self-consuming, to lie dormant
for the rest of a lifetime. You disdain such sophistry:
absence must mean more than that. And yet
I find the hackneyed image of ruined life
too close for comfort, anatomy turned to *ash*, my life
as *Music Hall*: would you, this missing year

have put a cool tongue where it burns,
with body-shade
                           tamed it for domestic heat?
By being here, together, spilling here

the juice that makes things grow, couldn't we
smother last year's calculation, and defy
the new round of tremors?

It is another year without family.
Our answer—we have not, will not become strangers—
is well known. Too well known.

I write to a house in a street,
your new setting, selective as a postcard.
We are, for the moment, tourists
exchanging notes. More than guilt drives us

back to where addresses coincide: I am recalling
a walk up the hill

to Cabris, our Cézanne village, lived in.

Up the hill from another village we learnt to spell
and, for a time, called home. Then, we were envied.
That Mediterranean ripening saw us through

cooler seasons, separation
to others. Across the sea we spoke, we *speak*
of the *coup* of saying
what the foreign tongue allowed, and of *knowing* the rest.
More than a little, that allayed fear
that we could be cheated, that had we lived

separated by centuries as well as by sea
we might not know this life together.

So in five days, or ten days, if there is no accident
you will open your envelope
and be on our terrace with a view of the sea;
you will marvel at the *oliviers*, silvery after rain;
with a friend, defy the sun
up the hill to Cabris—the cicada losing its menace
from the famous poem: in your hand *l'asperge*
growing into lunch. Somewhere in this letter
will be the early-morning smell of *croissants*
and a swim, nearby, where people whom the world knows
have swum.

These are not attempts to nudge memory,
not straws that friends glance at, guardedly.
They are yours, without this letter. They speak
of shared address, a suitcase left, a plan for home.

2

'Why do you want to fight wars? It is not amusing.'
—a Stockholm friend

Now this year's address says nothing to you,
nothing of me to you. I think of postcards:

Wish you were here. All speak
English here. They tell jokes
in the shops. The jokes have
little to do with their lives—
that, perhaps, keeps them
cheerful... Love.

But this is a card to someone encountered
at work, at an amusing party; or perhaps
further back in history—a fellow sufferer in the Plato

seminar, or in numbing hours translating
Beowulf; someone defying probability after two decades
rising now to middling eminence. This card

is for such a twice-a-year acquaintance. It is not yours.

3

'...Apart from religious ceremonies, triduums, novenas,
gardening, harvesting, vintaging, whippings, slavery, incest,
hangings, invasions, sackings, rape and pestilence, we have had
no experience.'
—Sister Theodora in Italo Calvino's The Nonexistent Knight

We are not the centre of the universe. Do not make
this statement for effect, it will fall flat,
your listeners will accept it. I have learned

to conceal surprise—as you your anger.
I sometimes think to go half-way and meet
those who will write the world's meaning

into separation—to make you less angry?
I hold the pen, but the voice, insistent, is behind
my ear... *Dear Comrade, Widow, Fellow-sufferer...*

> *...they have come again...in the night...*
> *and have gone away, like last night*
> *empty-handed.*
> *Professionals; they will not kill till*
> *they are ready, rather cannibalize the Will*
> *to resist. They aim to prove me unappetizing*
> *harvest of the hurricane, the mistral, green-ripening*
> *to no purpose... Conscious again, I take care*
> *to block out the rest, the coming fear*
> *with, yes, a walk up the hill between our villages*
> *picking l'asperge, safe in private languages*
> *not in this letter.*
> My love.
> (It is better.)

They make me say this. I let them.
But no more. You are in a strange place.
You cannot be sure how much of this is cheap revenge

on the past. Do not over-react.

4

You do not recall last year in Spéracèdes, in Cabris.

(...It was not last year, you're growing literal. Two,
three American Presidents have, as they say, risen
without trace. Our own obscurity is worse, it has
no cushion of sympathy, of gloating, of contempt...)

No, you do not recall that last year in Spéracèdes,
in Cabris: I am a messenger, then, with unwelcome news.
Those who, like us, sojourned there

have moved on. Unlike us they took care
to drive piles into the stubborn mountain-side
and now sprout children. They, like us

went through the motions, tying up the vines
picking the courgettes, learning ancient craft
with stones on terraces to prevent our patch
of *Alpes Maritimes* sliding into sea.
That was another life, you say, an address
better to forget: these letters are like children's
balloons running out of air. So my next note
must break a window or pull you up short,
like a terrorist in the body, with a knife. Our life
in the village, I say, is at risk. Others
went through the motions but

                              unlike us, paused
at a tempting vine

and *bruised* it, in a private place.
They packed earth in a hollow stone
and watered it. They diverted the stream

to a secret terrace, and with springwater
wash what now looks like a baby's face. Their *public*
lives, only, wear suitcases like ours...:

they leave Spéracèdes, they leave Cabris
with more than luggage. They have no need
for letters soggy with memory.

 Let us be angry at the same time, and act together
united in this annual letter to our friends:

Dear folks,

 I hope you are well, hope that this year's vin
rouge still rots the liver. Hope you can
find contemplation on your hillside
despite over-building, still see Cannes
in the distance. Love, as ever, to your summer tide
of drifters, buoyant with concern for those who starve
as they slowly, expertly, empty the cave.

5   (a letter from Albania)

Some have been returned because of their obviousness.
Neither of us now is known at his, at her address. It is right
that fastidiousness drives us into hiding. Stray and fading
memories add indignity, only, to a half-life, misspent.
But for the drug which lures me to the more perfect, more
remote place from which to say, 'Come home', I would not

still bother you. Like any addict needing more
to restore the dye of memory, I blunder into

secrets:
                    (Assassinations, Revolutions, far-away
wars are part of what those who live
live with)
                    Have I wandered off the map?

                                        Week Two

My Love,

Here we are back in Durrës, on the Adriatic coast.
Sunday. Diplomats, mainly 'Third World', on the beach...

A resort, built by Russians before the big breach
let China in (& out). Hotel too large for its
size; candelabra in the dining-room; on hands and knees

women keep it clean. Our guide, Naim, who sees
all, finds no contradiction in this 'Naked Ape' scene.
An alert, intelligent man, he talks of Albanian gold

43

stolen by Britain: what to expect from old
capitalists? He is not angry, just vindicated
that a country with racism as its leading industry

no longer needs him to condemn it in the eyes of History.

Tuesday

One of our group, a moody lad who came on a dare, doesn't
like it much. None of it. The Thousand Stairs of Gjirokastra,

the famous white cheese, isn't a patch on his native Leicester.
But there are compensations; yesterday's trip to
raw-faced Korça, new flats for its 60,000 inhabitants,

uncovered what we long sought, our first dissidents,
schoolmaster & (absent) wife defying the Party, calling
a halt at two children. And more, allowing the younger

to use her 'dextrous' left hand to write. But stronger
logic than we display—he warns us, he is no 'wet'—is
    needed
to resolve the contradictions we call *choice* (For what

it's worth, that conversation took place not
at Korça where the tourist 'ruin' was Turkish, but in leafy
Elbasan. Lamb for lunch. Good cognac, too). Would you say

to a child there were *two* ways to walk? That is to play
with life, the man said. But enough. Talking of play, *Look!*
right here in the town, you can see Shakespeare,

a shrewd Englishman to set his Comedy in Illyria,
our homeland, hedging, as you say, his bets. And is it true
that whites in England black their faces, like cheats,

making the real Othellos play out their parts in the streets?
He is sorry, he seeks only information. I am a guest, we must
enjoy the scenery, the War Memorial, Roman Ruins...:

44

Friday

'*Lateral Thinking & West Indian Sport*'
—Essay by A.E.N. Von Hallett on a proposed
Grenada-Albanian Cricket Match

'*The Art of Government is Pushin' up you han', Pushin' up you
han' and then bowling a straight ball*'
—Cricket enthusiast, Sturge Park, Montserrat

the country

is like Montserrat of an earlier decade; the hoe, the odd
    donkey...
but for mountains with Party slogans, the tidiness
of everything, children scrubbed and well-behaved, larger

than their parents. Another success for Comrade Enver
    Hoxha
breaking the centuries-long cycle of malnutrition.
Thinking we're a Delegation, people wave; we feel such
    frauds

and want to help with the harvest. We elude our guards
as they seem; but spring-onion fields are out of bounds
this year. So are the bunkers, each with its gun

to defend Democracy, not for jaded tourists' fun.
(Be warned, Yugoslavia, and others with dollars and
    roubles:
heroic soldiers holding hands in the street, strong

and unselfish, know how often Albanian freedom must be
    won.)

Week Three

A change of driver to the Capital. He's been abroad
but still does his annual spell of 'productive labour':

45

he can drive, but we suspect him of being in High favour.
Tirana. Looking down from the hotel on Skanderbeg
   Square,
a Lowry scene. Then to the Atheist Museum where
   ex-King Zog

vies for ignominy with Popes, U.S. Presidents and other
   relatives of God.
Unreal without cars; people dwarfed by the Palace of
   Culture;
Chinese bicycles, Chinese jokes... In time, we see a pram

pushed by a foreign lady, and a non-Albanian man...
Love.

6   (a letter not sent)

'We met the enemy, and he was us'
—General William Westmoreland on Vietnam

Why should I tell you that fascists and torturers
are alive and well—to divert attention from ourselves?

My love, I hope your new kettle turns itself off.
Our last adventure with a kettle served us
privately with such stories as others dine out on.
I should not like you to duplicate such intimacies...

My love, step back from the passing car, my hand
on your elbow; cross the square at night, only in dream,
to break up the fight. Do not get killed
should you cross with your eyes open

as we did at Ebertplatz, adding years to life:
(do you need a decade's rest after such lunacies together?)
My love, do not stop fights in the street. Unless...
No, fake innocence, selfishness, youth

and deal with the bad conscience at leisure:
it is irresponsible to die while fascists and torturers etc. etc.
So there. Do not read foolish letters. Ignore them.
Change more than your name. Go to live in another century.

                                        My love.

4   The House in Montserrat

Village Remains—Old Man

(born c.1865)

Don't blame me:
when against the run of play
someone scores
let the losing team worry.

You get my meaning.
When the wife
good & true
though generous to a fault
but in all other senses
man of the house,

when she
in breach of custom, dies
leaving me exposed
less-than-half,
the stunted cotton-tree
in a family of weeds—

do you expect a new crop?
The old days back?

Talk of decline had its uses:
here lies the player
who failed the team
still flirting with rules
of the wrong game.
Then graduates came
with theses of Reconstruction.

Now root-gatherers, clearing, prying
discover me here
unrepentant (no hero,
no lost leader in waiting),
the house in ruins,
children's children

precariously abroad.
Don't blame me:
I never was in charge.
Too late by decades
to check *diaspora*
in the drawing-room
dictionary;

or to mourn a clever half
more safely dead. Indelicate,
really, in a relic
from that house of promise.

Don't Talk to Me about Bread

she kneads
deep into the night
and the whey-coloured dough

springy and easy and yielding to her will

is revenge. Like a rival,
dough toys with her. Black-brown hands in the belly
bringing forth a sigh.

She slaps it, slaps it double with fists
with heel of hand applies the punishment
not meant for bread

and the bitch on the table sighs
and exhales a little spray of flour
a satisfied breath of white

on her hand

mocking the colour
robbing hands of their power
as they go through the motions, kneading...
She listens for the sigh which haunts

from the wrong side of her own door
from this wanton cheat of dough
this whey-faced bitch rising up

in spite of her fight, rising up
her nipples, her belly, rising up
two legs, dear god, in a blackwoman's rage...

Laughing at her, all laughing at her:
giggling bitch, abandoned house, and Man
still promising from afar what men promise...

Hands come to life again: knife
in the hand, the belly ripped open, and she smears

white lard and butter, she sprinkles
a little obeah of flour and curses to stop up the wound.

Then she doubles the bitch up
with cuffs, wrings her like washing
till she's the wrong shape

and the tramp lets out a damp, little sigh
a little hiss of white
enjoying it.

A Little Ritual

I wake you at the right time,
your water ready and bubbling with ash,
the yard smelling of kerosene, the cock too startled to crow.

I let the animal kick me as you slit its throat;
steady it, hold up the lamp
as you scrape it clean, string up and jackripper

like the expert: before daybreak we have meat.
I wash the spot clean of evidence
wash you feed you love you clean of evidence...

Now the yard is silent, pig comes
in packets and kerosene lamps went out with you
when the yard died.

And I wash the spot clean of evidence
and love you as you wish
in the past tense.

Nellie in the Bread Room

The lizard scuttling through grass
mocks us both, like a mechanized arm,
or animated toy set to scud
over private memory. This is your room,

the Bread Room, back when the house
was alive. The sky is blue, everyone younger
by a quarter of a century, and you are caught
in a pose we remember: you hold

the flat-iron an inch from your face
to test its heat; and satisfied, make the swap
in the coalpot. The thud thud
of sheets being ironed nails down the stillness

of afternoon into something more permanent
than childhood. Not yet the rumoured thrill
of changing seasons, the promised gift
of snow. Heat: the heat censures

any mood more urgent than restlessness.
From the Animal Pound, greenish-sweet fug
of coalpit soothes like a collective
cigarette. Even the spurt of crowing

from a cock quickly muffles in a flutter
of wings, a scratch of feathers. Mr Frederick,
inching up the hill in time for dinner
will never have to hurry. Now what crawls here

rejects our stale, sea-stained memory
of sweetbread, fruit ripening on trees
named after the family, of freshly-laundered
pride and a piano abusing the afternoon for an hour:

this house, hurricane-proof
built for a free great grandmother
to be born in has served part of its purpose.
Why pick on Nellie's room—one only

of twelve, invisible assets smuggled
abroad to be frozen in a cold country? Time,
left behind, didn't stop there. Like the bookcase
in the drawing-room, whose bindings are too faint

to read; like Ruby, grandfather's horse
surviving him by a decade, or small secrets
of four generations, the House eludes
both us and History. Yet they walk out of your book,

figures from the village coming to fill buckets
at the water-trough, to grind cassava
at the Mill, to bake bread. The ironed cloth
unfolds as Sunday linen on the table inviting

a man with an Irish accent, a vicar, to lunch.
Somewhere, calming a hurricane with prayer,
is grandfather. Everywhere, here, grandmother
presiding over all, too wise to have predicted this.

Late Return

for Howard Fergus

'What an odd name, Markham, for a Montserratian!'
—Canadian tourist in Montserrat

'There is no Markham in the Directory.'—Telephone Exchange

i

The ruin, at least, was something; the yard
with face half-rutted was the boy no girl would kiss
except in retrospect; blotches of soil erupting
like teenage lust: a tangle of green—sugarapple,
mango, sour now, outgrowing the graft of family name;
other fruit, near-fruit...
With no young scamp to lizard vertical for juice,
your nuts are safe: weeds cling
in parody to trunk (like boys born after you, tall,
or long-abandoned sons made good, defying dad
to wish them better) unharnessed
by Nellie's line on which the great, white
sheets of the house would flap their wings in rage.
Fringed Afro of arrogance:
their better view of the sea taunts us, close
to earth, flaunting fruit too high to get at;
some beyond-the-milk stage bunched as if in decoration.
Well before dark, my challenge from below, half-
remembered, no-more-to-be-taken-up, peters out:
mine is a garden, not of Eden, but of youth.
Suspecting things to be as honest, as accurate as they seem,
that this bit of family, untended, past its best
season, reflects something in me, I reach
for the camera I don't possess. Someone in Europe,
in America, will find this quaint. For me, a tourist-
polaroid to arrest decline.

ii

I am home again, perhaps two generations late.
I think, when the jumble of accusation, of longing,
clears: I am the juvenile not yet exiled.
This rock is a springboard
into water, into sea.
Sea is safe mattress
for the pole-vaulter, beyond sand;
my ocean-liner, vast and reliable, absorbing
shock, proof of completed journeys near to risk,
knowing the way to 'abroad'. The jump
is voluntary as coming to a road which forks:
sudden pressure from behind makes you choose
without benefit of signpost. Now this:
Montserrat has caught up with the world,
impatient of late-comers, of its children, foreign-ravaged,
straggling home without humility. (High-flying
Concorde boxing people's ears is enough.)
Others have been unpersoned
through the idiocies of politics. I, who seek no public
cut to advancement, am an Economic
not a political dissident.

Familiar picture: Man & suitcase,
contents not from this place; professional migrant
eyeing the landscape. My unpaid guide tells a story
of a potato patch, a villa-patch cleared
too soon. A riot of green is the penalty.
Less young in energy, we must try again.

iii

Later, second thoughts come to the rescue
and puncture self-conceit: things affecting you
affect not only you, etc. 'Most of what matters
in your life takes place in your absence' is a verdict
with the threat drained out. (In that absence, woodlice

59

ate your house.) But something of you
lives here, a voice not heard in twenty years,
stubbornly locked in the present. The mind,
like a cat's paw, tries to trap stray cloud of memory,
mists of past, raindrops thrown by an unseen hand...
Inevitably, it locates you in the third person.

Is he a late developer?
He was sure of it, then, hot afternoons
stumped by Latin homework, bowled by the Physics
master before he took guard, before he was ready.
At home, out of the team, without Excursion
to Antigua to represent the School, he had to make do
with books; books one day, hopefully, to be swapped
for passport. Here, he watched the ants

materializing from nowhere
to attack the remains of lunch. He thinks—
Regam Reges Reget...: Such communication systems
    grow out of...
Amabam Amabas Amabat (Uncomfortable, the
    imperfect tense)
Amavero Amaveris Amaverit...

(What is the consequence if I do not kill these ants?)

His colleagues halfway to Antigua to play the big match,
he imagines he sees them, ants on the boat. He can
advise them. Ivan's late cut is dangerous. At trials,
Ivan *twice* cut the ball in the air, and got away with it:
Five runs. Ivan will be caught in Antigua before he
    scores...
Capio Capere Cepi Captum... Were we ants, boys
from School, we would find a way
to cross sea,
get message to Ivan. These ants, he notices,
place information above life: what makes them do it?

Could it be they love one another? Too foolish
a notion for a boy early in his teens
who didn't make the team, and must settle for Latin:
Amavi Amavisti Amavit.

He thinks:
after the bombs, will the ants be here?
(Maybe he has not become a scholar
to sustain such thoughts.) He thinks of a passport
stamped, stamped in Antigua, stamped in the next island,
stamped here; luggage searched, questions asked,
and is not ashamed of the obvious:
absence of love. We haven't learnt from the ants.

iv

Again the question: do I unpack?
(Releasing echoes of *Wanderer*, of *Seafarer*, of *Salesman*,
1st Generation immigrant hawking knick-knacks
at the door? Do I hope to dazzle
for an hour, a week, and move on? Isn't it here
that others, with my history, have underestimated
their capacity for low goals?)

To unpack or not? The case represents
all the skill I have, success, over the years
of reducing the contents of many into one—
like absorbing disciplines into a single brain
(Nellie must have felt this way, here, after the first
cassava-bread: reaping the root, peeling, washing,
grinding at the Mill—man & boy treading pole—
the white, poisonous cassava piling up in its box, its coffin...
Over-night Press; sifting, baking on hot plate:
thin, light cassava-bread.) What of this remains
in my case?

The opened case, inevitably, won't close.
A moment of panic: could the fart of Concorde
on its way to Venezuela be luggage you can't leave?
No, this is man-menopause, faking new consciousness.
I no longer wish to prevent bits of Montserrat
smuggling in

though night sounds of crickets and dogs weigh nothing,
bats no longer have a house to be blind in;
Scots at the Agouti, Canadians at Vue Pointe
travel lightly in my head. The biography that grows
and grows in my baggage, started life a pamphlet, an
    underlined
name, a literate slave at Riley's reading the declaration
of emancipation. Nincom has filled the years
since 1834, and my case won't close.

And more: under the bathtowel, samples of beaches
still free to all. Here and there, memory of kindness,
of beauty, verbs of local colour TO DANCE TO SING—
    TO LOVE ?
They belong here: is it crude of me to smuggle them
into that dark place where part of me still lives?

A History Without Suffering

In this poem there is no suffering.
It spans hundreds of years and records
no deaths, connecting when it can,
those moments where people are healthy

and happy, content to be alive. A Chapter,
maybe a Volume, shorn of violence
consists of an adult reading aimlessly.
This line is the length of a full life

smuggled in while no one was plotting
against a neighbour, except in jest.
Then, after a gap, comes Nellie. She
is in a drought-fisted field

with a hoe. This is her twelfth year
on the land, and today her back
doesn't hurt. Catechisms of self-pity
and of murder have declared a day's truce

in the Civil War within her. So today,
we can bring Nellie, content with herself,
with the world, into our History.
For a day. In the next generation

we find a suitable subject camping
near the border of a divided country:
for a while no one knows how near. For these
few lines she is ours. But how about

the lovers? you ask, the freshly-washed
body close to yours; sounds, smells, tastes;
anticipation of the young, the edited memory
of the rest of us? How about thoughts

higher than their thinkers?... Yes, yes.
Give them half a line and a mass of footnotes:
they have their own privileged history,
like inherited income beside our husbandry.

We bring our History up to date
in a city like London: someone's just paid
the mortgage, is free of guilt
and not dying of cancer; and going

past the news-stand, doesn't see a headline
advertising torture. This is all
recommended reading, but in small doses.
It shows you can avoid suffering, if you try.

The Widow

i

take the midnight taxi to her bed
through the bodyguard of
bats and restless insects,
before next year's abandonment of the farm...

the throb of diesel fills her room with—
do not think it—no longer prone,
she's on guard to exile husbands—friends
who return and keep the engine running.

She's wary of more blood, explanations
of a grim and far-off War-in-progress
that has widowed and romanced her
linked her with the lover who comes in taxis
to report...

comes to hold her to a promise
that widows can be urged to make.

These not-quite husbands on long nights between
their wars, will probe for supply of wifely conduct—
dry walls that shore up childhood landscapes to let in
new prowlers through the gaps that others made escaping:

she must reoccupy abandoned spaces, chasms between
the crumbling
comfort of respect
and her widow-fear of vertigo—these near-husbands
like childhood fruit-trees ripe with summer
give the lie to barren landscape, impregnating
(O sweet, uncensored non-fascist badverbs), irrigating
with surplus sap, flooding all her mouths
raw and wet with the farm night's body-juices.

Do not appeal to witnesses (before-the-drought friends
    roasting
sweetcorn, killing chickens, burning
the cassava bread—
                    chopping up stunted mango-wood in
                    farewell).
Rivals now, they wear in the sun, the ragged
conscience of old clothes on a stick in a ploughed potato
    field.

ii

The taxi, waiting with comfort in the darkness
with rescue from an exile
throbs out the message of its master.
Safe from cattle-truck, meat-lorry, blacked-out van
the widow shudders under impact: it has been worse.

The waiting taxi is expensive
in the morning, clocked and packed
(her mangoes and bananas are permanently out of season)—
packed with cardboard boxes and a case or two of
    scrap-book memories.

Chock-full, they will say, stacked by mistake, the work
the mess of amateurs in haste: a mugging in the night of
    love...

and in the morning (why not admit it?) she,
widow-wise, will be barren like a trampled field
her bed-stained cloud of memory—like a spot
in the yard where the goat, perhaps, was slaughtered—
memorial only to an ancient feast

And she will attack the washing-up with violence
sniffing it for diesel.

The Three Sisters on a Tropical Island

They're part of the flock of snow-birds
flying South for the winter, coming
to permanent roost here:
Olga, Masha and Irina who even in New England
teaching, marrying, remarrying
still dreamt of return to Moscow.
Olga's advanced spinsterhood reeks
authority over fickle, messy sisters
guilty (ah, they never could be American)
about wealth unearned by work work work
imagined in that house of their first innocence.
Justifying partners who think the cavalry
something primitive, no match for guns
and computers, who strain to leave widows rich,
is behind them—a late-adopted country.
Masha, at least, has killed her Kulygin
with kindness, admitting him in Boston
to her lovers whose fierce
intelligence drove stale pedantry hard
into retreat and text-book Latin: dog-devotion
to the woman still his wife, intact. It was a relief
that this husband, dying, loft her no money.
Irina, like a lady in fiction, still wears
her white dress. Tempted, on the death
of the Baron all those decades ago,
to change, she declined such over-statement
of Love: she would not compete with a married sister.
Now her hair has come to match the dress,
and black is the colour of their adopted
country. They have seen Russia and America—
that's how they tell it to visitors, at night
on a terrace overlooking the Capitol—
and have discovered, at last, Paradise.
The villa is spacious
as memories of their youth: what more
can three ageing sisters want?

They still weep, of course, and ask
one another why. Not for Moscow, not—
O please not for dear brother Andrew
who could have been, should have been
Professor, had not insufferable Natasha
read their fortune, had he not
allowed her to marry him.

Family Matters

for my mother

'God is very generous, He ignores us most of the time'
—Toni Morrison in conversation

i

Strange how late in life Love comes
to be your sort of word. Silly to distance it
with fake regret for that moment
when the man old enough to be her father
saved himself from ridicule, finally.
A word loaned to others, the long-standing couple
growing past self-interest into friendship
sweeter for their surprise in it:
the flicker of regret at life underlived
was yours, the good taste not to hanker, theirs.
Now, your word, returning home.

This mask of detachment fools no one.
The word is mine, I will use it.
I am thinking of a woman, part-stranger to my habits.
Starting out ahead, she planned the rendezvous
on some horizon where our interests would meet,
if not our minds. The generation—
or any other—gap was not foreseen,
while we were adding to the house,
calming fears about genetics, stray sheep, History,
packing for unsure status abroad.
The time to say Love was missed.
Boys who inherit Schools say it in Latin:
the *mater* crowd. I'm not one of them.

ii

Better to answer other people's questions
than be condemned to your own:
What Shall We Do About Mutti?

Mutti is next-door neighbour's
ubiquitous cat; *Mutti* is the harmless
joke at the family get-together
circling above today's troublesome
member, self-conscious as the...
'Shall we go S-W-I-M-M-I-N-G?'
or 'Who would like an I-C-E-C-R-E-A-M?'
games of childhood. The child
in question, orphaned early by a husband,
will not appear to be concerned
with *Mutti*. Her whiff of home
sets you on the edge
of temper for what was squandered—
clutching, like small change,
your decision-making status.
It's one of your duties
to be paternally rational, to smother
unease. You tantalize the game
with brooding and discover, say, that *parent*
is less the unfashionable suit you didn't choose
than skin you're still wrapped in.
All this is understood. And so,
behind conspiracy of eyes, you ask again:
What shall we do about *Mutti?*

Together, we wonder why what they call Progress
Has eluded us. She expects me to do more than guess

At an answer, a scholar with his book.
Others managed in half the time it took

Me to emerge from the learning-jumble with furniture
Fit for Sotheby's. She will not add her stricture

To others; we are alive, we must not seem
Ungrateful, must not dwell on what-might-have-been.

A picture in the newspaper catches her eye,
A famous actress as a girl: we must all die

It seems. But how to square this beauty
With the raddled woman just buried? Our duty,

She would have said in earlier, firmer days
Is to be ready. But alone now we avert our gaze

From what threatens intimacy, fill in
With snippets from the newspaper, live within

Madonna & Child constraint found in no Gallery. She
    deserves
A private bath, a cruise on QE2, all which serves

As palliative for me, not her. More honest to exhibit
From my book of 17th-century plays, young Allwit

Saying something quaint and amoral, till the TV News
Intrudes and forces us to choose

Between children in and out of uniform facing death for us.
Her response here, indifferent to race, is more generous

Than mine. Relief, yes, to feel inadequate again
As years before, in a minor test of memory when

She won out over our new telephone number. Very well.
Here she is, Queen in exile, learning not to dwell

On treachery of those of us renouncing her line.
God, she says, helps. She wishes me sons to maintain mine.

iv

'I must do my homework to make Germany strong again'
—a young Köln student

A guardian, you preserve from an upstairs window
three or four generations, in memory
unlike eyesight and hearing, too stubborn to fade.

Out of reach, below, are the girls;
one, two generations late, yours: her mother,
punishing you, took her *kalashnikov* to a grievance.

Self-conscious at mixed shame and pride
you accept the new Front Line drawn
at your gate: the girls, tough as their time

have graduated to homework. They do not flinch
from the newspaper face battered
into grown-up business.

Your habit is to pry
till you feel the catch in the stomach,
see a suspect huddling violence, cross the road.

He is summoned by your phalanx of five-year-olds.
They have not learnt the lesson of adults.
They revive old fantasies of life before risk.

Under the bargain window money changes hands,
and the threat moves off with a Get Well Soon card
in his pocket. The *Avenue Five*

have done their bit for the local victim savaged by thugs—
a word they use without blush. Upstairs,
memory toys with a partner who clings to it: the girls

are like him and will grow into talk and impotence.
Then again, like the absent not-quite wife & daughter
who early in life learnt to shoot straight

impatient of a bookish uncle's grey areas;
and demanded a clear target
and relied on others to keep confusion out of the way.

Who said an old man's memory was reliable?
He can shut the window, snap the link between generations
and stop mugging new life with doubt.

Over There

Here, when the fresh cut of abuse
falls into an old wound, Over There
comes to the rescue; hot springs & sunshine, the family
putting its head together under a threat,
coming up strong and defiant as Uncle George's laugh,
bruised by malaria in Panama, disappointment in Haiti,
now frozen into myth.

More in respect than grief, parents take to the air.
In the interests of school I am let off
the funeral; but soon learn how Over There
is changing better into best;
is catching God in a good mood
developing and brightening up the place—

though with the old quaking rumble in his stomach
and other crudish side-effects. The great
wild storms of temper still uproot trees
and leave people homeless; but that
is a compromise you can live with: different
here, the grubby hand of hate

setting fire to your house. Can I claim
what they claim, a place so far, its fruit and vegetables
go quaint on my plate, where even footballers
come out playing cricket? Over There
is where parents go to bury family
and come back lighter, for a day or two, bouncing
round the house, as if they're still young.

5 Games & Penalties

Today

The blur of last night's television
the shapes that cushion other people's nights
the ticking of the morning headlines

wrap me securely.
Today I am bomb-proof.
This is new, but expected.

I curl round another antidote and
whispers kiss over my head
so I do not bruise.

I am inside.
Everything is inside.
There is no outside.

Mouths shut firmly.
The ball is a head
is a boil

ripening.
The bomb ticking
is me.

New Year 1982

Time for tired, old resolutions
you don't quite make, the agnostic
and his religion. Yet you can see
no particular value in being perverse.

To be less brutal—if that's
the word—less meish
to the few who gamely suffer it;
and add to those Conspiracy Theories

yourself, past 40, alive
with no knife-scar, qualifying then
for privilege. The year has freed
its surfeit of surgeons

without their tools. Over-eager,
they use what comes to hand: cigarettes,
bayonets, they use hot wires, they use bullets.
We sort out which are ours

and sigh with relief when the names
prove foreign, difficult to say: we always knew
it couldn't happen here. We take cue
from newsreaders

who pronounce Poland in that attitude
of secular prayer, that tasteful
posture between virtue and guilt. Amen:
we are better people than our lives allow.

In the newspaper, on an inside page
away from the crises, a filler. The woman
has been seen before, and yes, she will live.
Far from husband, family, banned

anew by the 'State', Winnie Mandela. Guiltless,
she has won the right to see the big fish
she married, twice a month, through glass.
Twenty-four years a couple, four staggered months

together: is there time to ponder
the dogma of interrupted lives? Winnie longs,
like a young girl, for the experience
of marriage. Once cruel and unusual

punishment now trimmed to an inside page.
Of course we turn over and find new armies
giddily practising surgery. Why, we no longer ask,
do these *Polacks* come to smother us each year?

Anonymous

At the wrong end of the room
my life waits for me. It's grown
attractive over the years, defeating
villains who would possess it.

Time to cross the room: the view
of the street remains alien so I must
reclaim what was never mine—
homecoming for the unloved.

Such journeys are more difficult
than words, and my room empties several
lives, as I get to the bookcase
pretending to need a book.

My life does not wait, but battles
with its villains to return
a little more soiled. Naturally
we apologize to each other

as I'm too embarrassed to leave home.
We fill the room with concern,
with souvenirs for evidence
of the world's untidiness

till I'm pressed against the walls
with you again outside, part
of the life of the street
which is still not mine.

As I grow smaller than the world
I haunt large rooms
in disguise and speak to
strangers as if they were strangers

and wilt early in the evening.

A Complacent Little Poem
Greets a Revolutionary Big Poem

Listen, think of something else.
The hose is being turned off, blood
washed away; the crowd, numbed
and guilty, won't witness it.

Safe now to write a little poem.
It will face up to the mess,
the broken bodies etc., and hint at something
darker. It will have a fighting title.

The Long Road from Bordeaux to Paris

(on having survived Mauriac)

She cycles into the dusk, ringing
her bell. Out of sight
labourers fall upon her, spilling
amid farm-droppings, seed
to grow like oak-trees in the village.

We lose her for a time, scurrying
North to shelter in the crowd
a world away.

There she is again turning off the boulevard,
off the edge of Baron Haussmann's
old map. A lover stops
her cycle, punishes and returns her to the husband

with apologies. We leave them there. Man & Wife
preparing another future
with olive trees instead of pines

and the rapes done differently.

Cliché?

Growing older? Funny how the years
stagger like over-loaded travellers

changing trains; the panting
man still conscious of his dignity,

of a lost morning fussing
to discover his face: he finds

himself late in the day contemplating
his navel—missing the trip.

Each day he determines to be more thorough
with himself; and discarding past

selves, starts—when he starts—further
behind. In time he repairs personal

luggage, makes himself recognizable.
What then? A visit to the library

before closing time, to learn
that younger men have managed

to get through their wars, their
headlines, on this derailed day.

a little poem

i

a perfect plastic surgeon, wig-maker and military tailor
an empty mouth, little heaps of teeth, gardening tools,
this year's Witch-doctor. Last year's Economist. The gun.

Etc. Wives, mothers, mistresses and so on; men: people
sitting in chairs, these complete the jigsaw and snub our
    little poem.

It will leap off the page with *anger*
...well, with relief, more or less intact—
one less patient-in-care, one vacant, soiled sheet.

Respecting your intelligence it will speak
with the challenging voice of the time
of one who has seen all, knows the right
answers; who will deny that your joint aim is manufacture
    of love-acid:

        and you are the witnesses
you were there when they came with axes
with fire, you heard the screams ('But some of my best
    friends
are torturers!') and escaped in fear and embarrassment
as another little bit of jigsaw hacked its way into your
    puzzle.

ii

and you are right to protest
to reject the finger accusing you
of cowardice, complicity, lack of imagination—
you who acquiesced as the little *nothing*-fragment
trimmed and labelled itself the 'brevity of wisdom'
claiming to eradicate another *ism* in 30 strident lines—

one of those poems to tickle your appetites, like a passing
   affair
before drifting off into *Myth*.

                 So now, safe, wrapped
in the white sheets of oblivion, why must you
be disturbed, be made to relive an old story?

When you were young and
under the influence of imagination, yes, the axe
bit into the door, the door splintered, splintered
like so many strips of paper from a mad Official:
you saw them take wing, flutter down, hover
overhead: they *squawked* till there was no other sound of
   torture.

iii

the creature with the broken back is a parody
of the poem you have come to know and love
and offends a little, like the brute without speech, *alien*,
who spits his mess about the room, like bricks,
like the toys of a child, bullying its adult
with little piles of teeth
      blooding its gum
          now a dentist with the wrong instruments.

This brutish creature upsetting the jigsaw of your pride
exposes you to new tests, the ridicule
of refitting
          your men into   strange women
your little heap of teeth   a dentist?
the teenager's mind the geriatric body   30 lines of poem?
the white coat in the laboratory   30 lines of poem
one empty torture-chamber   One well-spoken Fascist
one meaning   so many words

one little poem trying to be something else.

Words Fit to Eat

I sometimes consider the possibility of being wrong
and not knowing it till I am left
with a warehouse of words which,
like old stock, have gone out of fashion

(unlike other fads of youth, they show no sign
of returning to favour): a salesman, then,

of nostalgia too proud to dump his wares.
Suspicious that he never was the man he used to be,
he must take his own advice and not hope
for miracles (he must pretend this always was
his advice) and take his penalty like a man.

And how will he eat his words? They are tough
and marrowless bones, not made for old men's teeth;
they have, in the past, been blunt weapons
whose jagged marks of hate, of injunction
frighten him now.

Ah, do not believe it, not all of it.
What of those other words, lines of them, shaped
by youth, by the tug of life, stacked in fun, in hope

with riddles for label? They have amused
stray shoppers and passers-by and still infuse an old man
with dawns he wished to see, with something bright and
    tropical—
unblemished skin, clean teeth, laughter.
But like a meddler, I have not allowed words

to be words, but shaped them like tools of a trade
which made those redundant who would not be retrained.
When the world was difficult, they were stones and bullets;
other times they grew plump and fat, like breasts,
like fruit, good to chew on, good to be with.

They made a virtue of being real
of ripening out of season, creatures of their time.
Better exchange them for imperishables neatly stored,
a dry mouth of jokes and riddles

jokes and riddles of the chicken crossing the road
of riot police looking up from their novels chanting
PEACE PEACE PEACE
of crude lines out of context, of other Life-tasks
    accomplished

like shifting Monday to another part of the week.

Looking round my warehouse I find much to eat.
But I am forbidden most things
my appetite is small.

Like the condemned man on his last day
I am tempted to be arbitrary, promiscuous and choke by
    accident
or to posture and eat the worst words I can find

and go out by my own hand.

Footnotes

LITERATURE & ART [1]
CULTURE & WIT [2]
CIVILIZATION [3]
MEMOIRS [4]
FOREIGNERS [5]
SOCIOLOGY [6]
RELIGION & POLITICS [7]

1:   a civilized plot
     by addicts of Literature
     to arrest content
     with a Form.

2:   A good joke. But
     for those without
     my true refinement
     I did not mean it.

3:   A success story.
     Of course, through friends
     I later repaired the damage,
     returned the kindness.

4:   I, like god, am seen
     to best advantage through
     my plan. But friends and
     detractors demand footnotes.

5.   The dream turns solid:
     a new weight on their backs
     from hosts who say, 'Pretending's
     no fun any more.'

6:   a doss-house where
     each new arrival brings
     for his keep, a Language
     that smells clean.

7:   towards Stability & Change where
     tensions recede, wars are qualified,
     games multi-cultural and swedish
     factories are housing-estates.

Pioneer

She must not allow herself
these fantasies—Postman, Milkman,
Dustman: they are like her, losers
in this new order as in the last.

And yet she reads of men like these
nursing resentment against odds
seldom in their favour: perplexed,
they yearn for scapegoats.

In this land where zig-zagging
notions of belonging breed anxiety,
who will jump the gun with a new
New Order, caring little that the end

is, as always, bodies under rubble?
New interests leave old allies
watchful: will they succumb to the thrill
of violence

and disturb her sleep with another night
of broken glass? In her fantasy,
the crazed succeed the cautious,
weak minds become drunk, and she

is on the other side, outnumbered.
So who will make himself *Oberlagerführer*
of the street? The Milkman
is plump and, in uniform, would be memorable

in a history-book. The Dustman's youth
and brusqueness reminds her of the whip
(We Have Ways To Improve Production):
She recalls Ukrainian women beaten

about the breast with rubber hoses
just twelve years before accident
(which some call Fate) set her down
on this Continent. She must not allow

herself these fantasies. The paper-boy's
Brownshirt is just a garment. The Postman's
joke is only to be expected—
from someone not properly brought up.

Intact

Sometimes it seems there are birds hovering
over her head.

Here she is, a stranger among neighbours concealing
their unease; and she having to put the case

for the new set: after being summoned
and again, by the regiment of experts
trained by her enemies

accusing the lady of quaint habits
not her own—after all this

and watching her sons grow into their father,
so dated in these fashion-conscious times;
after losing the way

to make words fit her as when she was young
and a finicky dresser— grand jokes, particularly
now beyond her circumstance;

after all this (though, suspiciously, growing
into old clothes again) she recalls, ah,
the wickedness

of new-baked bread recurring every morning,
each crust snug with its body like the right time of life,
brown and healthy:

in the shop someone impersonates the morning,
the sniff of bread triggering little bursts of laughter
into the air

And suddenly the crows of her exile are no longer there.

Mammie

She would hold up her head though
fresh air still slapped her
about the face
as if she was an immigrant.
She should know better than to gate-
crash at her—now unnecessary—
age, a garden reserved to residents
with a future.
But a little bit of memory returned
to sit with her
to share a *past* with her
and prepare a joke she could use
against her exile. The ships
which brought them here had seemed
proud and confident, mistresses
of the sea. Now they too
were scrap.
              A familiar wreck adrift
in the city where her husband
went missing, berthed for a moment
like a man from home. She was pleased
he was not the father of her sons.

Penalties

No one is having a breakdown in an upstairs room.
Down here, we accept one another and make
small adjustment to our bodies.
There is one breast missing since last time,

and we fancy we don't know which
without ungallant probing, without disturbing the memory.
At dinner we are unfussy, passing over
the pork, a persistent vegetable, the nearer

of two wines; yet we eat modestly and hope
others take heart from this.
So here we are again—not quite the same
people, but from afar, near enough. Here we are

after twenty years or so, my eyes not quite seeing:
across the table, her fingers in his hair, stranded
without hair. The young wife fills
a gap and does it well. Strange to think that one of us sitting

here is dead. In panic someone will seize
his neighbour and hurry off to make, well, love.
Just in case. And we part thinking ourselves reasonably
in luck. When next we meet another one of us will be
    missing.

And we are now, older, dreaming of replacements.

The Night of the Short Knives

Suppose then we celebrate:
the scratch on the door at midnight
is now past history. And knives
in the Alley are far from us.

I hear you say: this is an odd
time, a between-the-histories time
for cleaning out attics, clearing
obstacles to restored good fortune.

Let us celebrate again
like survivors rediscovering patterns
in the carpet they have looted: ugly
stains enhance the treasure, after cleaning.

The bowel-moving earthquakes
of the past, twisted metal
of man-made trains and aeroplanes
from which we have escaped, still unsettle

like friends unmarrying themselves.
Suppose we confront the armed man
in the Alley, and claim Right of Theory—
even as we hit the pavement?

94

The Cost of Sanity

(an English Myth)

We are friends here laying bare
what isn't flesh: we accept
our clothes. Elsewhere
allies defect, leaving gaps in our judgement.
Better to go on meeting like present company.
Better to cover tracks.

This is sanity, not to reach for the world's
blanket of dismay. (In this garden
no one defaults, though I had not thought till now
to hang the mood 'desolate' on this autumn.)
Like friends of long standing, perhaps like strangers
at a party, we can still tease
a phrase that tenses us.

We are in the garden of a friend's home.
Inside, there is famine on a wall. Murder too:
a child, pregnant in a foreign drought. Here, in the garden,
a friend copes, bending to observe what looks like grass:
'Tell me, is it happy? Is the plant happy?'

A Good Day

Her first day out
and about

in the Spring
as promised.

Across the road
a man, his stride unhurried, hands
behind back

handcuffed.
Ah, yes, he knows

his weakness
and today will resist

temptation. No one
is so crude

as to introduce them.

The Sea

It used to be at the bottom of the hill
and brought white ships and news
of a far land where half my life
was scheduled to be lived.

That was at least half a life ago
of managing without maps, plans, permanence
of a dozen or more addresses
of riding the trains like a vagrant.

Today, I have visitors. They come
long distances overland. They will be uneasy
and console me for loss of the sea.
I will discourage them.

Infiltrated

Still possible to say them aloud, these words
which came without thinking
which fitted onto the page as words should
looking neat, tamed by their order.

It was easy to deny they were anything
but words, to be glanced at, to please
the eye like the well-kept hedge
or chinese characters on a wall seen

from the bus. So I hold them up now in public
and through cracked gaps of defacement
glimpse the squalor, the fact that squatters
have long been there. Words lost

to their echo: a scarred and blackened
little hedge—tramps aping soldiers
in peacetime, unlucky to be sent to war. There goes
with them... all that is not left of me.

Travelling Without You

i

The temptations are real enough,
to recognize blood gradually turning to vinegar:
sourness is something I can live with.
So, there we are, then:
one tortured body survives its twin;
a mind interfered with goes shrieking to the funnyhouse
or remains to confound us with its ordinariness.

There's a time of life, they say, to pause
and acknowledge these things:
it's the plateau where Tomorrow begins to lose its threat
and real age seems a generation's walk away.
Here you can admit you were less bright than was thought,
and make light the lack of credibility.
If only the partner were here
to mock these sermons,
this lecture-hall posture, to mock
in that special way of couples good together, the pretence
that much was expected of you when young...

Do not overestimate this plateau-stop.
It affords illumination only
to those susceptible to miracles. The rest of us
unwrap imagination and discover in *you*
armies to be led, a god to be tamed.
We have come too far to fret over nothing.

ii

Why aren't you here?
Commonsense and the manuals agree
on this meeting halfway.
Life is still too short

to retrace steps, to correct mistakes
of past error.
Up here, exposed, adolescent,
the graham-greene Character loose in adult wilfulness,
I expect you over the horizon, soiled,
demanding romance as a right.
I have learnt, now, to dance.

Years of waiting, shedding youth
and avoiding accident and illness
have paid off. You will scan my body
for knifemarks and be suspicious
that all still seems so clean.

iii

There are worse places to be than here:
everyone in the world must say it. High ground
brings more of *now*
into view, ironing out disappointment, marking
'lost chances' with barely a break in the footpath.
Friends who didn't make it—the mismatched couple—
no longer seem like the time's failures:
they settle on the slopes, no uglier now than the rest of us.
Ah, but you don't want sermons from me. Better
to clown a little and say with hindsight—
that travelling without partner can't be clever
when those less stubborn seem to make it together.

6 Lambchops, Philpot

Lambchops B.A.

And after the cricket when the ball was lost
and the lads sat around discussing the past

scores, disowning the team, matching lists
of old heroes, then came a bit of politics.

And what was this new trick in a grave situation
to be tossed a few middle-aged B.A.'s in compensation?

Well, it was our lot to do time, running the trains
cleaning up the country, being apprenticed to new games;

but now we're on the march again, they say
unite with superblacks grooving on a B.A.

It's Lambchops's turn then not to be outdone
with his briefcase and dark glasses at the B.M.

Now he can fart in comfort twice a week
between a puzzled nun and a black aesthete.

Lambchops Goes into Training

Chateauneuf du Pape; German/Hungarian/Yugoslavian
Riesling; Côtes du Rhône/du Provence, Cyprus

Sherry—that's not the half of what he's giving
up for the Contest. He must also say NO to his

better-half of a dream Sociologist, NO
to self-abuse to the *Sun* and *Mirror* sin-page.

But Crusades have never been won by compromise.
He must nail the lie once and for all—of feck-

lessness, lack of application, racial special-
pleading. The early-morning jog through

the park, six weeks on the building-site
and regular arm-wrestling have done wonders

for the body. But the *mind*, Lambchops, needs
muscling up. His strongest rival is a woman

using Psychology to unnerve him. She is out,
they say, learning to piss at the roadside without

wetting her shoes. It's been tried before,
darling, it won't wash. Lambchops will learn

to play chess, to count in Yiddish, to recognize
Mozart. He will be *complete* for the Contest:

body of Muhammad Ali, mind of a great Cynic
and Chinese all over—with the world's computers

date-matching him. Training over, he relaxes
with a Shakespearian Sonnet, and stays awake

pondering the strangeness of things. Why for instance
do they need to use knives tomorrow for the darts match?

A Mugger's Game

Chase him down the alley
put him behind bars

in a basement and charge him rent.

Lambchops has potential
for violence. He's faking,

says the Pig in the wig,

make him an example
of our collective self-defence.

Black them here stop them there

before they get too cheeky
too second-generation aware

and ape us overtake us

queueing up for houses
they claim their fathers built.

They're a problem so he's a problem

a potential mugger
on a quiet English street,

so smash him smash him

or soon he'll flash an education
and leave you crumpled in a heap.

Lambchops Protests
with His Person-Friend

So this holiday there will be no house-
decorating, no moving of old fridges,
no overtime; all because of the new person-

friend. Lambchops undresses to emphasize
his protest—a good start to the holiday.
Since then, our man has middle-aged

three days. Shampooed, Lambchops announces
a Spanish breakfast, for wheat-germ
has no national boundary while dictionaries

are at hand: today, Spain/Italy/France;
tomorrow, the World. While the person-friend
makes her own statement on little bare

feet in pavement shit (anyone can perform
on the beach), Lambchops writes the postcards
so as not to tire her, washes up, cleans

the bath, and is anointed with conjugal
vitamin E to saturation—her overfed
baby. But she's a true double-

graduate and approaches the unknown
with skill and confidence. Privileged,
she's been educated to like the factory-

worker, and has become Lambchops's higher
form of life, his macrobiotics Lady. She goes
for walks and brings home soya beans &

miso-wakame seaweed to mix with sex & poetry
and the I Ching. What's she like then?
his friends ask. What's she like

at the moment of impact? (Bert's little girl
used to come screaming in *Turkish*
which nearly sent him back to his wife—

that's why he's at night school trying
to improve his love-life.) What is
she like, thinks Lambchops, dressing-

gowned, lotus-positioned, decaffeinating
(by accident? by design?) his soreness. She's
like a holiday taken at the right time.

Lambchops Wrestles with His Love-Letter

For it has to correspond a little
with the person, that's the trouble:

cross-eyed and bow-legged: not
much joy there... And how can you manage

not to mention the bad skin? 3½
teeth missing, and the ½ hasn't hurt

for twelve years. 'Leave well alone,
I always say.' But she's normal

in spite of it. No hangups. *Then start*
with the lack of hangups! She looks

inwards and reasonably likes what
she sees: a sensible girl who uses cosmetics

from necessity, not vanity.
Safe and dependable, a clean-eating

young wife opting for a non-violent hobby.
Her whole-wheat smile, functional

kissing, and good digestion demonstrate
28½ off-white teeth to be adequate

for a normal low-budget life. And the root-
beer-barrel legs? Well, they come in handy,

don't they? for the back-rubbing.
Dear... tropical plant of the High Street...

Lambchops's Ally

Now is the summer of his disrespect.
He passes oncoming women on the left
disdaining a glance at the hopeful strip

of breast—he's been five hours now past
indignity, and still carries before him
(like a fireman's ladder at full stretch)

the weight of his first printed poem—
an arrow in the crowd. Earlier,
it was love at first sight when the ladder

was a woman, their snatched moments straddling
breakfast had not yet turned into a duel
of ego. Yet he should have known

she was false and betrayed him finally
with an Editor, now to return
less prized than before. But once

out of sight, she again filled his mind—
a tight shelf of books in the Library,
attention at a reading, *introduction*

to strangers—a phallic ladder losing its end
in smoke. Now, now these merciless women
have turned their breasts away, are giving

him back his poem—an ex-wife at his side turning
her lack of cleavage, his lack of height
into a fighting matter—a *pre-five-hour*

cliché. The challenge comes like an accident
and he stumbles (why won't the poem fight?)
but rights himself under the ladder

down which fans in nightdress clamber
from the smoke. He administers to the wounded
allies. He appoints the poem bodyguard.

Ode on the Death of a Rich Man

Lambchops apologizes for never having
written an ode. He apologizes

again for the literary lie. But
he was young then.

Now, his thoughts on hearing
of the death of a rich man—

considering the poor who go singly,
tidily, obey merely the Law of Nature—

his thoughts on hearing that the man died
finally

leaving so many well-paid doctors and expectant
wives stranded

(as well as Brothers and Sisters
mourning their god

for loss of service)—these thoughts mug
an aimless poem

into nastiness. And now, in order to teach
other rich men—and their servants—

a lesson, Lambchops thinks
he might attempt an ode.

A Slow Developer

53 paces down the street
(53, you're doing fine). STOP:
on the right, one floor off
the ground, is your brother's
room—and yours. Why

are you bleeding? The house
cannot be climbed, is not
your coconut tree. Use the key,
man, use the key. THE KEY
will not fit the door today.

The sigh, unlike the blow
means it's bad but not that bad.
You're doing well, my friend,
you're doing fine. You've got

the *number* right, but the *street*

LOOK-AT-THE-NAME-OF-THE-STREET!

Black Man's Curse

Halfway through the weekend, the fun
starts: we're on our knees like a couple

of perverts checking out the bedroom floor
(only, she objected to this image, which left us

crouching like private detectives on heat):
it's the little black hairs we're after—

stubborn rascals getting everywhere—from bath
and wash-basin to tell-tale places

in other rooms—even the odd book
or magazine I happen to have glanced through.

I'm just a multiple walking clue. Even
without the haircut, the little squealers

keep watch for the Man. 'It's moral
blackmail,' says the Lady, tense and angry,

'it's as bad as old-fashioned guilt.' But
we were on the wrong side of a thing

so much bigger than both of us, turning
it all Platonic. There was little time left

for anything but the removal of evidence,
of suspected evidence, of non-evidence;

till the lovers' reprieve suddenly came through
turning all the black hairs grey.

It tinged of the Man's sense of humour—
this kind of Divine Intervention.

People's Summit

First, it was to be held at his—the man's
place—the out-of-work man. But Maureen's chief

adviser objected: is that a concession Kissinger
would make at the start of negotiations?

He demanded new terms of reference which saw her,
who paid the rent, as hosting the Conference.

His Lawyer's speech was commended by all, and led
to the first adjournment. Lambchops's pad was ruled out,

he being co-respondent to this thing; and as not
to lose the impetus, they decided to meet

in the local underground on a Sunday morning.
It was what you would call a triangle kept in shape

by the pressure of advice from outside. They were
all poor people in a difficult situation, whose

choice of action was limited. Suicide and other
heroic solutions were out. Duelling was from

another tradition: why couldn't the three live
somehow as one, or maybe two? But these were

civilized people—and fastidious. The brilliant
Lawyer commended Africa's traditional winner-

take-all development policy: did we three lack
Africa's courage? The West Indian thing was

Compromise-and-let-the-three-live sort of thing.
Whether this was a good thing (that thing again)

objectively, was something they adjourned to think
about. Lambchops said, to solve this one was to delve

through the false bottom of West Indian ambivalence
to the bed-rock on which our great nation of the future

must be built. But Philpot thought it feeble
of Lambchops to turn politician just to win a woman

like Maureen. And so it went on. Advisers got bored,
changed jobs and families, left; but over the years

the triangle managed to keep something
of its original shape; for it's a big decision

when you come down to it, and poor people
can't afford to be wrong all the time.

Progress

The woman is older and taller
than him, that's progress.

Horizontal, but unyielding: over-
cultivation, drought and years

of neglect have turned her into desert.
Water, she knows from experience,

washes dead soil away, laying
bare the skull of rock. She

will preserve what she has saved
of herself. Away with progress.

But a little moisture in the right
place; strange, stiff fingers

of the plough and seeds like historical
immigrants to overflow the land

have made the desert bloom.
The woman radiates green field,

grows full and confident
and herself threatens rain.

The woman, like a ripe tree, bends
to feed him. Progress.

A House-Husband Called Philpot

Perhaps he should paint his toenails today
and be one with the women. There are no

children to vegetate to, no race of males
to liberate himself from: he has bought

the time his talent demanded, and talent
sneaked away leaving him exposed. Neighbouring

house-husbands with time on their hands, drop
by to debate issues of the day, the big

questions of life, like getting into a Lady's
purse, or into her bed—and ways of being good

to their women, out at work. Certainly,
this sort of training (in place of child-

bearing) has kept his friends from turning
into cabbage. Later, the women will blame them

for that. But as always, there's the catch.
Childhood acne has followed him into middle age:

it's his personal wiping-the-baby's-bottom curse
as blood and matter spurt on the mirror, leaving

his face, well-repaired, a mass of scars and ruts
and scabs of differing colours. How could *she*

come home to such a mess? He will paint his toe-
nails after all. That might divert her.

Adult Education

Gone is the stack of *Playboy*,
Playboy substitutes, assorted nudes.

Philpot is determined to break
the habit: unlike the ex-smoker, he's

on his own. He looks back on a time
before he was addicted, and can't remember

it. He's been adult all his life
yet his pleasures, they tell him,

are those of a child. He has vowed
reform so often, his friends

dismiss him as a comic turn. But this time
he's determined to take the 'You're

never too old to learn' joke seriously.
Surreptitiously, Philpot opens his first

textbook in forty years, defying
Maureen and regretting the two or three

kind women not eligible for the class.
'What do you say after you say Hello?'

the book asks, on the front page; but
there are no pictures, and the new

student will have to read through
200 pages to find out.

Appeal

It was his age, she thought—
a vulnerable time when the glance

of a 17-year-old on the loose
spelt trouble for the household.

Maureen knew this one was big:
the man was trying too hard—like

pulling in his stomach when friends
arrived. What could have caused him,

a foolish, thoughtless man
to donate a pound to a stranger's

brain operation? Philpot
didn't want to seem stubborn, alien:

if he had transgressed against some ethnic
Law, or just gone soft in the head,

he would impose his own sanctions.
He determined to check up on his

investment, to find out what form
of life he was helping to prolong.

And if the family in question turned out
to be fascist—would he have to demand

his money back? And would his pound
still be clean? There should be a Law,

after all, against 17-year-olds on the loose.

Philpot Puzzled

'There's someone else', she says,
sitting opposite him tracing

with a finger too elegant
for his wife, patterns on the oilskin.

She is speaking, not to or at Philpot
not even *through* him, but slightly

over his shoulder; and the sentence
comes from someone other than Maureen.

'There's someone else' is a guest
in the house replacing her, discarding

her life's '*A goin' dance wid Roy.*
Expec' me when you see me' language.

He's afraid to touch the newly-
elegant finger which is not hers;

and searches for a suitable phrase
of submission to match his new status.

But it doesn't come. He is still
pondering, alone at the table, giving

the impression of a defeated Philpot
who doesn't care.

Queueing

Philpot responds to the touch
on his shoulder, a friend
in the slow-moving queue.

But it's a different hand,
more recent, replacing
a previous queue-dweller.

What are they trying to tell
him, friend and stranger alike?
Have earlier ones broken

the line? Have they lacked
endurance and fallen out,
died? Refusing to panic,

Philpot acknowledges his new
friend, marks his own spot
again, and watches for movement.

Philpot's Progress

'He stared at her with envy
as if she was something
he could not afford to buy.'

He stared at her wondering
why she evoked that image,
thinking it no longer true.

He blinked away the embarrassment
of Philpot the skiver finding
his doctor sick, of Philpot

growing deformed, a broken-
off, discoloured toe-nail
in his hand.

Now he was like a driver,
short of his goal, about to reverse—
for winning always turned into something else.

Crossing the Fence

(Thoughts of a First Generation Immigrant)

It took a long time to accept
that he was here to stay—in this

old body which he'll now have to keep
for the rest of his life;

and that he'd die in this country:
that his last great wish would be to go

peacefully. Trips to the Greek Islands
weren't for him. Supersonic travel

was a spectator sport; yet the British
Rail Express from Euston to Manchester

was consolation of sorts. Engineering
and Art and the price of his vote

had turned the coachwork into a poor man's
Concorde, a flight of imagination

with space for luggage. Surely, he was
being conveyed more graciously than ever

Queen Victoria managed: had he mellowed
into thinking there were degrees

to poverty; that being able, say, to exchange
the canefields of youth for inner-city manhood

was a *plus*? On his way to the loo he noticed
an ugly rent on one of the seats

and two smug-looking truants sheltering
behind the generation gap. Suddenly,

a distant war had spilled over into
his territory, and Philpot was going to fight.

Middle Age

He considers the possibility
of growing old and dying
without violence.

               The children
will have to be brought together
like unwilling pets

before running off again
in the normal way. The wives—
the wives must be rolled into one

large unfamiliar woman,
resenting it, accepting it,
knowing this is the way

of nature with her class
and sex. They'll settle in
a house with a wall and gates

left over from the last tenant;
and some will envy this image
of people dying peacefully.

Philpot & Bertha Krupp

In his absence she would work
to maintain their business interests

and live up to the German name.
That's why he left her a young widow

in the tradition of the family.
Now she must be Man of Iron, Man of Steel

with a young son or old husband
and elevate the house to something new.

Philpot would challenge fortune and defy
the Lawmen: return to Montserrat, his ancestral

Essen, was overdue—there to restore Villa Hügel
to the 1950s, Mammie's time.

He could not let the last Thirty Year War of Migration
which had diverted all their energies

contract his hopes. (Was this wise? Will they
be happy? That was an old Doris Day song, pap

for the masses.) Back here, the woman
would play the part of any formidable

Krupp Bertha, refusing to lie down
in the wake of circumstance. Don't tell him

Maureen would opt for a role of immigrant,
the one-parent creature of Public Opinion

confirming him in her malice, to die
like old Gustav, helpless, dumb and senile?

The Potato Patch

In those days there was a god,
and the thought rinsed her mind leaving

it clear: had the island disappeared
with its god? Certainly, she'd never

see either again. Would her potato-
patch be recognizable after 20 years—

what shape would it be, eroded,
at the bottom of the sea? Maureen looks

at the window-box of her new flat
and knows someone has played a practical

joke: will there be a hoe in the broom-
cupboard, a pig or bearded goat tied

to the bus-stop outside, waiting
to be fed? The last tenants were city-

bred children obeying their private
call to nature: would their potatoes

turn up at the local greengrocer's
and remind her that she was far from home?

Notes

Life after Spéracèdes

p.44   *raw-faced Korça:* It is thought more important to embark on the next building than to use up valuable resources putting the expected 'finish' to the one under construction; hence the raw look to new buildings in most Albanian towns.

p.44   *the dissident headmaster:* a) A person of the headmaster's status would be encouraged to have a large family to meet Albania's population growth target. b) Right-handedness is a sign of orthodoxy in Albania. Thus, left-handed children are forced in school to write with their right hand.

p.47   *Ebertplatz:* A part of Köln where several nationalities meet. Occasionally the excitement is more than you bargain for (see 'The Night of the Short Knives').

Late Return

p.62   *Agouti* and *Vue Pointe:* Venues of island night-life. Agouti, rough and ready; Vue Pointe, sophisticated, upmarket hotel entertainment.

p.62   *Nincom:* A literate slave at Riley's estate who. on 1 August 1834, was invited to read to the assembled company the Declaration of Emancipation — and did so with ease.

The Three Sisters on a Tropical Island

p.67   It's easy to imagine the Sisters journeying not to Moscow but to the West and, finally, coming to rest on a tropical island.

Family Matters

p.70   *Mutti* is a diminutive of *mutter* (mother, in German).

Footnotes

p.88   *7:* Written towards the end of a spell of Swedish pragmatism, in Stockholm.

Philpot and Bertha Krupp

p.124   Philpot tries on roles as some people do clothes; occasionally, they fit.